BASKETBALL LEGENDS

Kareem Abdul-Jabbar
Charles Barkley
Larry Bird
Wilt Chamberlain
Clyde Drexler
Julius Erving
Patrick Ewing
Anfernee Hardaway
The Head Coaches
Grant Hill
Juwan Howard
Allen Iverson
Magic Johnson
Michael Jordan
Shawn Kemp
Jason Kidd
Reggie Miller
Alonzo Mourning
Hakeem Olajuwon
Shaquille O'Neal
Gary Payton
Scottie Pippen
David Robinson
Dennis Rodman
John Stockton

CHELSEA HOUSE PUBLISHERS

THE HEAD COACHES

Josh Wilker

Introduction by
Chuck Daly

CHELSEA HOUSE PUBLISHERS
Philadelphia

Produced by Daniel Bial and Associates
New York, New York

Picture research by Alan Gottlieb
Cover illustration by Bradford Brown
Frontispiece photo: George Karl

First Printing

1 3 5 7 9 8 6 4 2

Library of Congress Cataloging-in-Publication Data

Wilker, Josh.
The head coaches / J. Wilker.
p.   cm.   —   (Basketball legends)
Includes bibliographical references (p.   ) and index.
Summary: Discusses the coaching careers of some notable
personalities from the National Basketball Association, including
Red Auerbach, Phil Jackson, Pat Riley, and Lenny Wilkens.
ISBN 0-7910-4580-3 (hc)
1. Basketball coaches—United States—Biography—Juvenile
literature. [1. Basketball coaches.] I. Title. II. Series.
GV884.A1W55 1998
796.333'092'273—dc21
[B]   97-42865
                                                                      CIP
                                                                       AC

CONTENTS

BECOMING A BASKETBALL LEGEND

Chuck Daly

What does it take to be a basketball superstar? Two of the three things it takes are easy to spot. Any great athlete must have excellent skills and tremendous dedication. The third quality needed is much harder to define, or even put into words. Some call it leadership or desire to win, but I'm not sure that explains it fully. This third quality relates to the athlete's thinking process, a certain mentality and work ethic. One can coach athletic skills, and while few superstars need outside influence to help keep them dedicated, it is possible for a coach to offer some well-timed words in order to keep that athlete fully motivated. But a coach can do no more than appeal to a player's will to win; how much that player is then capable of ensuring victory is up to his own internal workings.

In recent times, we have been fortunate to have seen some of the best to play the game. Larry Bird, Magic Johnson, and Michael Jordan had all three components of superstardom in full measure. They brought their teams to numerous championships, and made the players around them better. (They also made their coaches look smart.)

I myself coached a player who belongs in that class, Isiah Thomas, who helped lead the Detroit Pistons to consecutive NBA crowns. Isiah is not tall—he's just over six feet—but he could do whatever he wanted with the ball. And what he wanted to do most was lead and win.

All the players I mentioned above and those whom this series will chronicle are tremendously gifted athletes, but for the most part, you can't play professional basketball at all unless you have excellent skills. And few players get to stay on their team unless they are willing to dedicate themselves to improving their talents even more, learning about their opponents, and finding a way to join with their teammates and win.

It's that third element that separates the good player from the superstar, the memorable players from the legends of the game. Superstars know when to take over the game. If the situation calls for a defensive stop, the superstars stand up and do it. If the situation calls for a key pass, they make it. And if the situation calls for a big shot, they want the ball. They don't want the ball simply because of their own glory or ego. Instead they know—and their teammates know—that they are the ones who can deliver, regardless of the pressure.

The words "legend" and "superstar" are often tossed around without real meaning. Taking a hard look at some of those who truly can be classified as "legends" can provide insight into the things that brought them to that level. All of them developed their legacy over numerous seasons of play, even if certain games will always stand out in the memories of those who saw them. Those games typically featured amazing feats of all-around play. No matter how great the fans thought the superstars were, these players were capable of surprising the fans, their opponents, and occasionally even themselves. The desire to win took over, and with their dedication and athletic skills already in place, they were capable of the most astonishing achievements.

CHUCK DALY, now the head coach of the Orlando Magic, guided the Detroit Pistons to two straight NBA championships, in 1989 and 1990. He earned a gold medal as coach of the 1992 U.S. Olympic basketball team—the so-called "Dream Team"—and was inducted into the Pro Basketball Hall of Fame in 1994.

THE CHALLENGE

In a hotel room in Detroit, Don Nelson got up from the basketball game he'd been watching on television and took a couple of steps toward the bathroom. Everything went black. When Nelson came to moments later, he was lying facedown on the floor. A rough year as a coach in the National Basketball Association (NBA) had just gotten a little rougher.

Nelson was one of the better coaches in league history. But even the best coaches have not been immune to the tremendous physical and mental strain of the job. Johnny Kundla, who won five NBA titles with the Minneapolis Lakers in the 1940s and 1950s, suffered from severe stomach ulcers. And Red Auerbach, who set a new standard of excellence for NBA coaches when he won nine titles with the Boston Celtics in the 1950s and 1960s, decided to retire as a coach

A haggard Don Nelson wipes his face as his Milwaukee Bucks are about to be ousted from the play-offs.

when he could no longer recognize the bald, pale, haggard man looking back at him in the mirror.

Nelson had been worn out by an ugly dispute with a talented young player named Chris Webber. Webber, upon joining the team as a rookie in 1993, appeared to be the kind of dominant player who could help Nelson finally win an NBA title. An NBA title would allow Nelson, the only man to ever win the NBA Coach of the Year award three times, to take his place among the greatest coaches in NBA history—men like Kundla, Auerbach, Red Holzman, Pat Riley, Lenny Wilkens, and Phil Jackson. But Nelson's dream player quickly turned into a nightmare. Webber clashed with Nelson so often that the Warriors finally traded him away. A few days later, Nelson was facedown in a Detroit hotel room, wondering how he had gotten there. When the blackouts kept occurring, he landed in the hospital with a case of stress-induced viral pneumonia. A few months after that, he was fired.

It is not an easy job. Nelson staggered away from the Warriors job looking like a man who had taken a methodical beating. The strange thing was, he didn't look that different from any of the 28 head coaches he had left behind. Hall of Fame coach Chuck Daly, working as a television commentator, once described the way most coaches look: "Their eyes are red and there are black circles under those eyes. They are physically exhausted. They are mentally drained. They look awful because they feel awful. Then you talk to them—and they sound even worse than they look."

Then why on earth, Daly was asked, do these men continue to do what they do? "It's an addictive form of life," explained Daly. "You put yourself on the line every time your team takes the floor." As if to prove Daly's point, in 1995 Nelson came back to put himself on the line as the coach of the New York Knicks. And as if to further prove how merciless is the plight of the NBA coach, Nelson was fired again before the year was out.

He left behind several excellent coaches who, like him, seemed to be on the brink of coaching greatness. One of these men, George Karl, offered insight into the lure of his profession with some offhand comments to the press during the 1996 playoffs. His team, the Seattle SuperSonics, was locked in a knockdown, drag-out battle with the Utah Jazz for the Western Conference Championship. The winner would earn the right (or was it punishment?) to face Michael Jordan and the stampeding Chicago Bulls, who had ripped through the playoffs after compiling the best regular season record in history. The fiery Seattle coach was asked how, if given the chance, he could possibly impede the Bulls' seemingly inexorable march toward an NBA title. How on earth could he hope to stop Michael Jordan?

"I'd love the challenge of messing with Michael's head," Karl replied. "Maybe we'd triple-team him. Maybe we'd start with [center] Ervin Johnson on him. Maybe we won't guard him at all."

The first four words of Karl's answer—"I'd love the challenge"—could serve as the motto of all NBA coaches. They love the challenge of trying to win on an almost nightly basis. They love the challenge of keeping personality clashes (like Webber's clash with Nelson) from wrecking team unity. They love the challenge of devising effective offensive and defensive strategies. They even love the challenge of trying to stop Michael Jordan.

The love of the challenge brought George Karl back to the NBA after he was fired by both Cleveland and Golden State. After these firings, NBA teams neglected Karl for years, but he did not quit coaching. He coached and won for a franchise in Madrid, Spain. He coached and won for a minor league franchise in Albany, New York. Karl's love of whatever challenge the game offered was so strong that he seemed willing and able to take on any job, anywhere. He'd coach at the South Pole. He'd coach on the moon. Unfortunately for 28 of the teams in the NBA, a job offer came not from the moon but from Seattle.

In Seattle, Karl got to work with the kind of players he was missing in his previous two NBA jobs, and the young Sonics, as passionate and emotional as their coach, soon blossomed into one of the league's elite teams. In 1996, the Sonics topped the Jazz for the Western Conference title. In the Finals they fell behind the Bulls three games to none, but still, showing the tenacity of their coach, they held together as a team and kept fighting. They bloodied the previously untouched Bulls, twice staving off elimination to force the series to a sixth game, where the Bulls finally prevailed.

Another of the NBA's better coaches, Rudy Tomjanovich of the Houston Rockets, never even wanted to be a head coach. "When I was a player," said Tomjanovich, referring to his 10-year career as an All-Star NBA forward, "I thought you had to be a lunatic to get into coaching in the first place." In 1992, Tomjanovich was perfectly happy with his job as an assistant coach. Rocket management, however, was not happy with the Rockets' performance under head coach

*Rudy Tomjanovich talks with
Sam Cassell as the Rockets
go down to defeat during the
1994 NBA finals.*

Don Chaney. Tomjanovich was forced into duty.

The team, 26-26 at the time of Chaney's dismissal, began to show signs of life soon after Tomjanovich took over. Rudy T did not try to manipulate his players with intricate psychological ploys, and his players responded favorably to his honest, frank approach. "They may not agree with what I think," he said, "but at least they know I'm not playing games with them."

Tomjanovich quickly began to approach the job with the kind of obsessiveness that had made coaches seem to him, in former days, like lunatics. "No detail is too small for him to worry about," said assistant coach Carrol Dawson. In 1994 Rudy T's Rockets won the NBA championship. Afterward, in the jubilant Rocket locker room, guard Vernon Maxwell exclaimed, "There are probably people around the league wondering how we ever turned into a championship team. Well, Rudy T is a big part of the answer."

The Rockets repeated as champions the following year. But despite his back-to-back titles, Tomjanovich is not yet generally regarded as one of the game's legendary coaches. Part of this is because many see the transcendent play of Rocket center Hakeem Olajuwan as the sole reason for the Rockets' success. Part of it is simply because Rudy T has not been around long enough to be thought of as a legend.

Tomjanovich could further secure a place among the great coaches in NBA history by fashioning the kind of long-term, year-in, year-out success of coaches like the Los Angeles Lakers' Del Harris. Harris, who began his NBA career as Tomjanovich's coach in Houston, lacks the crowning achievement of an NBA championship, but for a decade and a half he has, in the manner of Don Nelson, pushed teams that lacked superstars into the playoffs. For only one short period did Harris have a superstar on his team. With Moses Malone (and little else), Harris coached the Rockets into the 1981 NBA Finals. Malone left Houston in 1982 as a free agent, and Harris was left with a team that played basketball as if trapped in a Three Stooges routine. The 1982-83 Rockets lost 68 games, and Harris was shown the door. It would be the only time in his career that his team would fail to make the playoffs.

He resurfaced in Milwaukee and for years kept a creaky team of aging veterans in the thick of torrid Midwest Division races. Harris adapted

Bill Fitch reacts to a muffed play during his first year as a coach of the Boston Celtics.

various strategies to battle Chuck Daly's bruising Pistons; Michael Jordan and the Bulls; the balanced, cerebral Cleveland Cavaliers; and the acrobatic Atlanta Hawks.

Harris further showed his adaptability when, in 1994, he took the Lakers head coaching job. The Lakers, unlike the Milwaukee Bucks, were virtually devoid of experienced players, yet Harris was able to lead the team into the playoffs in his first year there, a performance that earned him the Coach of the Year award. In the summer of 1996, the Lakers acquired Shaquille O'Neal from the Orlando Magic. The move instantly transformed the Lakers into a legitimate title contender. Anything short of a championship would be considered, by many, a failure. It's the kind of pressure-filled challenge that only an NBA coach could love.

Los Angeles's other team, the Clippers, are not title contenders, nor have they ever been. Bill Fitch, their current coach, was repeatedly asked when he joined the Clippers why he would want anything to do with a team that had been so consistently atrocious. Fitch had built winners all over the league, first in Cleveland (where he won the Coach of the Year award), then in Boston (where he won the NBA championship), then in Houston (where he took the Rockets to the NBA finals). He had nothing left to prove, and many wondered why he didn't simply ease into a richly deserved retirement. Why enter the endless Clipper nightmare?

"I like challenges," said Fitch, the quintessential NBA coach. "I looked at the Clipper job where so many other guys had failed and I thought, 'You know, there is a mountain no one has managed to climb. Maybe I can be the guy.'"

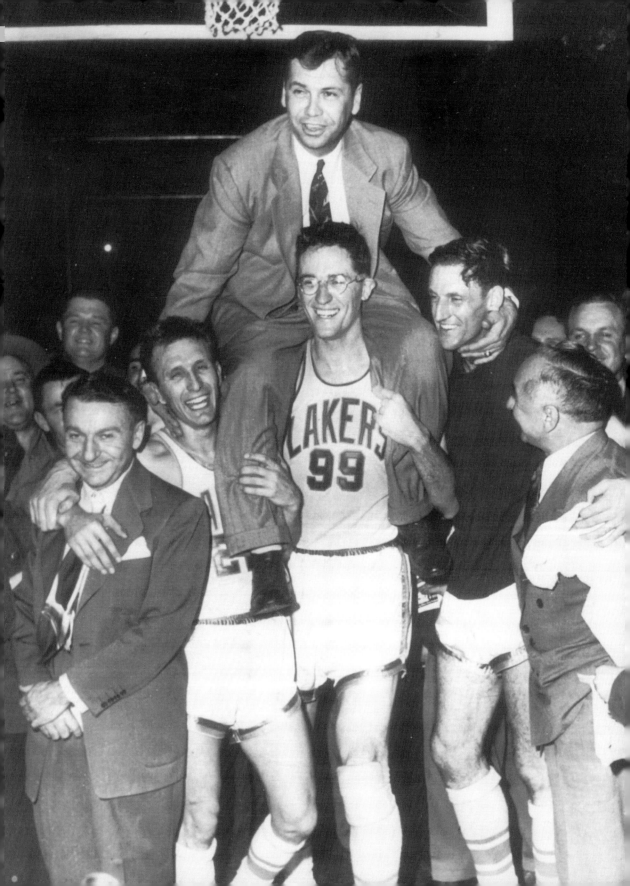

2

PIONEERS AND VISIONARIES

Four games into the 1947-48 season, the newest member of the Minneapolis Lakers, a 6'10" center named George Mikan, lumbered into the locker room for the first time. He was not a particularly graceful man. "I thought," recalled Lakers forward Jim Pollard, "that was the biggest-looking dumb character that I'd ever seen. . . ." The coach of the Lakers, Johnny Kundla, saw something more. He took one look at Mikan and instantly envisioned a way to achieve victory.

At that time, there had never been a dominant big man in professional basketball. For the first half of the century, all the best teams had put a premium on smaller, quicker players. Most coaches did not believe that a slow-footed man-mountain like Mikan could be the foundation of

George Mikan carries off Johnny Kundla after the Minneapolis Lakers won their fourth title in five years. Here also are Max Winter, the Lakers general manager (left), Slater Martin (number 22), Jim Pollard (in sweatshirt), and Lakers president Ben Berger (right).

a championship attack. Johnny Kundla did not, like these coaches, look back to the past. He looked forward, to the future, and in doing so laid the blueprints that NBA teams are to this day still using to win titles.

Kundla built the Lakers around Mikan. Mikan turned out to be unstoppable on offense, a scoring machine when close to the basket. He also was a dominant shot-blocker and rebounder on defense. Kundla, however, made sure that the Lakers were much more than a one-man team. "He did a great job of molding the team, taking care of the players' idiosyncrasies," said Mikan.

Kundla got the most out of each player's unique talents by devising specialized roles for each of them. In doing this, he further distinguished himself as a pioneer of the pro game. Before he came along, the two guards and two forwards on a team had been virtually interchangeable. This is not the case today, when the norm on a team is to have a point guard and a shooting guard, a small forward and a power forward. Kundla's Lakers were the first team to have players who filled these more thoroughly defined positions, with the quick and savvy Slater Martin at point guard, Bob Harrison or Pep Saul at shooting guard, the high-flying Jim Pollard at small forward, and rebound-scarfing Vern Mikkelson at power forward. These Lakers won a National Basketball League (NBL) title in 1948, a Basketball Association of America (BAA) title in 1949, and four NBA titles in five seasons from 1950 to 1954. After leading the Lakers to the NBA finals one last time in 1959, Kundla decided to heed the ominous ulcer pains in his stomach and retire.

Kundla's coaching career began winding down

around the same time the undistinguished NBA
playing career of a journeyman named Alex Hannum was ending. Midway through the 1956-57
season, as he sat the bench for the St. Louis
Hawks, Hannum's days in uniform appeared to
be numbered. But he wasn't the only person
associated with the struggling team in grave dan-
ger of losing his job. The coach, a man named
Red Holzman, sensing that the end was near,
tried to motivate his team with a somewhat dras-
tic action. "Toward the end," recalled Hawk center Charlie Share, "Holzman gave us a pep talk
where he pulled out pictures of his wife and kids
and asked us—pleaded with us—to win so that
he could keep his job and feed his family."

Despite the desperate speech, Holzman was
fired soon after. Star guard (and former Laker)
Slater Martin convinced Hawk management to
make Hannum the new coach. The aging bench-
warmer had been dangerously close to joining
Holzman in unemployment. General Manager
Marty Blake recalled, "We either were going to
make him a coach or put him on waivers."

The Hawks rallied under Hannum, winning
their way into the 1957 NBA Finals against the
Boston Celtics. The team benefited from Hannum's willingness to draw ideas from the minds
of his players. "After games," said Share, "Alex
would take guys out for beer and he'd talk over
the games and the team. He wanted to know
what we thought, and there were times when he
did change things."

Hannum wasn't afraid to try unorthodox
strategies. In game seven of the Finals, with his
team down by two points with two seconds left
in the game, Hannum devised a play in which
he would throw a full-court ricochet pass off the

backboard to Hawk forward Bob Pettit. The bizarre play yielded an easy shot for Pettit, but the Hawk star's jumper rimmed out.

Pettit would get a chance to redeem himself the following year. Hannum's team met the Celtics again in the 1958 Finals, and this time the Hawks were triumphant, led by an otherworldly 50-point performance in the final game by Pettit. It would take eight years before anyone else would find a way to beat the Celtics—Boston then reeled off one of the greatest winning streaks in sports history. It took until 1966 to find a team able to knock off the Celtics—and when the Philadelphia 76ers managed the feat, they did it with a coach by the name of Alex Hannum.

Hannum convinced 76ers star Wilt Chamberlain, the most unstoppable scorer the league has ever known, to play a more team-oriented game, and Philly, after setting a record for regular-season wins with 68, roared to the 1966-67 NBA title. Hannum added to his legend two years later by winning a championship with the Oakland Oaks of the renegade American Basketball Association (ABA). He remains one of only two men to win championships in both the NBA and ABA (Bill Sharman is the other). And Hannum is the only man ever to win NBA championships with two different franchises. He is most remembered, however, as the only man able to beat the Celtics during their otherwise unchallenged dynasty. In 13 years, the team in green failed to win a cham-

Red Holzman implores his team to do better in one of his last games as the Knicks' head coach.

pionship but two times, both to an Alex Hannum-led team. "Why did we finally beat Boston?" said Chamberlain after the 1966-67 season. "Because we had Alex Hannum as our coach."

Few coaches enjoy the almost immediate success of an Alex Hannum or a Johnny Kundla. A more common experience for the beginning NBA coach would be the one Hannum's predecessor in St. Louis, Red Holzman, suffered through. After the Hawks fired Holzman, he swore to himself that he'd never take another head coaching job again. He became a scout for the New York Knicks.

Holzman had the rare ability to see whether or not a certain young player would be able to mesh his own talents into a larger team concept. The Knicks began to climb out of the cellar of their division (where they had dwelled for years) as Holzman brought in talented, unselfish, hardworking players such as center Willis Reed, guard Walt Frazier, and forward Bill Bradley. But the Knicks did not become a serious contender until Holzman was persuaded to take over coaching duties midway through the 1967-68 season. The man who had assembled the team proved to be the perfect man to lead them. The Knicks finished strong under Holzman in 1968, and in 1969 they further announced their arrival as a force to be reckoned with by blitzing the division champion Baltimore Bullets 4-0 in the playoffs. Bullet forward Jack Marin said afterward, "It's unbelievable the way they hit the open man."

Holzman implored his team always to look for the open man on offense, and in the 1969-70 season the Knicks elevated his instructions to an art form. The ball zipped from man to man all over the court until the beleaguered, confused defense fell a step behind and a Knicks player was able to break into the clear. That open man would automatically get the ball, and a moment later the net would be dancing from a dead-on jump shot. Holzman's teams played a free-flowing, rhythmic, soulful game that did not stifle but enhanced whatever the individual player brought to the floor.

It was a joyous way to play ball, and it was often virtually unbeatable. The Knicks reached the NBA Finals three times in four years, coming away with the championship in both 1970 and 1973. "They were unselfish, each member of the team playing his role as orchestrated by Red Holzman," said current NBA coaching great Pat Riley. Riley then was a reserve guard for the Lakers—a Wilt Chamberlain-led team that was one of the Knicks' nemeses during their glory years. "As a player who competed against them," Riley said, "you could truly see five men playing as one."

Chuck Daly, like Red Holzman, had his share of difficulties when starting out as a coach. He got a chance to lead an NBA team only after a long, hard climb. He started out as a high school coach, worked for years as a college assistant, for years as a college coach, and for years as an NBA assistant. And when he finally did become an NBA head coach in 1981, it was with the flagrantly horrendous Cleveland Cavaliers. Daly lasted 41 games, 32 of which were losses.

Daly got another chance in 1983, with the Detroit Pistons. The Pistons had endured six straight losing seasons, but Daly transformed them into a playoff team. And when the high-scoring Pistons were quickly eliminated from the playoffs three years in a row, he transformed

Alex Hannum (center) celebrates after the 76ers beat the Warriors in the 1967 play-offs. In the back row (left to right) are Dave Gambee, Wally Jones, and Hal Greer. In the front row (left to right) are Luscious Jackson and Wilt Chamberlain.

them again. Daly wanted to win it all, and he knew what kind of team it would take to do that. "Defense wins," he said. "Defense travels. You win on the road with defense. There are nights when you are in New York and you left your jump shot back in Detroit. That happens. But a good team will take its defense with them onto the court every night, 82 nights a year."

Gifted defenders such as Dennis Rodman, John Salley, and Joe Dumars were added through the draft. The Pistons also acquired a backup forward/center named Rick Mahorn from the Washington Bullets, who joined the team already branded with the sinister nickname "McFilthy." Mahorn was the dirtiest player in the league, and Daly's Pistons followed his lead. The Bad Boys—as the team came to be known— elbowed, kicked, tripped, stepped on, bit, punched, blindsided, undercut, and did everything and anything else it took to win short of pulling a hunting knife from their shorts and stabbing their foes in the ribs.

Basketball purists vilified the Pistons as if they had in fact committed murder on the court. What the team's critics failed to see was that, beneath all the nefarious shenanigans and fisticuffs, the Pistons were, like Holzman's much more elegant Knicks, a consummate team. When they won the 1988-89 NBA title they became the first team in nearly three decades to do so without having a single player average more than 20 points a game.

The player who epitomized the team's willingness to sacrifice both their scoring average and their bodies for the good of the team was Rodman, whom Daly characterized as "the most unselfish player in the history of the NBA." In later years, when Daly was no longer his coach, the emotionally volcanic Rodman would gain renown as the player who was found mumbling to himself at 5:30 in the morning in a parked truck, a loaded shotgun on his lap; as the player who would earn countless suspensions from the league for misbehavior on the court; and as the player who showed up to a promotional gathering to publicize his autobiography wearing lipstick, eye shadow, and a wedding dress. It was to Daly's immense credit as a coach that he was able to keep Rodman's mind, and the minds of all his players, squarely focused on the game.

Daly, who won a second title with the Pistons in 1990 and led the "Dream Team" to a gold medal in the 1992 Olympics, took a selfish band of misfits known as the New Jersey Nets to the playoffs two years in a row. He retired after realizing he would more easily walk on water than lead the Nets to an NBA title. (In 1997, after working as a television commentator for a few years, he was lured back to coach the Orlando Magic by the promise of a big contract.) According to a candid Nets player named Jayson Williams, Daly need not hang his head at this. "I don't think Jesus can coach this team," said Williams.

3

RED AUERBACH

For the fans at Boston Garden, game four of the 1987 NBA Finals had not ended well. Lakers guard Magic Johnson had scored on a running hook shot in the closing seconds to beat the hometown Celtics and give his team a commanding three games to one lead in the series. It grew very quiet in the old building after that. If not for the insistent and grating voice of a stocky, balding, 69-year-old man, it might have been possible to hear a pin drop. It might have even been possible to hear the sound of the Boston Celtics' 16 NBA Championship banners shuddering in the drafty rafters high above the court.

But Red Auerbach, just three months shy of his 70th birthday, was not ready to go down quietly to defeat. The man who had played a major role in all 16 of the Celtics' titles (as head coach

---

Red Auerbach relishes a basket in the final minutes of the 1965 Finals. His Celtics were about to win their seventh consecutive world championship.

for nine and as team president and general manager for seven) stormed the court just after the final buzzer to harangue the official timekeeper and the referees. His argument, that the Celtics had been cheated out of the win, struck many as pointless poor sportsmanship. While Red Auerbach may not have been the best sportsman in this case (or ever), he never did anything that was pointless. He was always looking for an edge. The belligerent display was actually a tried and true Auerbach motivational ploy to create the feeling that the entire world was ganging up on the Celtics. The following game, an inspired Celtics team rose up and thrashed the Lakers. "People are telling me, 'Take it easy, the game's over,'" the leader of the Celtics said after his on-court quarrel in game four. "The game," he said, his eyes narrowing, "is never over."

The game, for the most successful coach in the history of the NBA (and arguably the most successful coach in the history of all professional sports), began in earnest in 1950 when Auerbach became the coach of the Boston Celtics. It was with the Celtics that Auerbach began to make the kind of moves that would shape a dynasty. Looking back on those moves, sports attorney Ron Grinker said, "He was so far ahead of the rest of the NBA. It was like he was playing chess while they were playing checkers."

One of Auerbach's first moves as the Celtics' coach was to draft a player named Chuck Cooper out of Duquesne University. The move made history—it was the first time a black player had been drafted by the NBA. Auerbach shrugged off any accolades for the move as brusquely as he had shrugged off the unwritten rule against drafting black players, saying simply, "I can honestly say he was the best player available."

Auerbach showed further that he was a man ahead of his time by going against the trend for snail-paced, half-court offense. He installed a revolutionary fast-break offense, and the Celtics, led by ball-handling wizard Bob Cousy, became the most exciting team in the league. They won plenty of games, too, but Auerbach saw that they needed something more if they wanted to win it all. He made a gutsy trade, sending popular high-scoring center Ed Macauley and a hot prospect named Cliff Hagan to St. Louis for the second pick in the 1956 college draft. With that pick he chose William Felton Russell.

Bill Russell, as Auerbach had envisioned, became the ironclad backbone of the Celtic fast break. He dominated on the defensive end as no one had before or has since, swatting shots and snaring rebounds and triggering the fast break with sharp, accurate outlet passes. The Celtics, led by their phenomenal rookie, made it to the NBA Finals in 1957 to face the St. Louis Hawks. Auerbach set the tone himself for what would be one of the more contentious and dramatic series in NBA history by decking Hawks owner Ben Kerner with a right cross minutes before the start of game three. The two men had been arguing at center court in the hostile St. Louis arena over the height of the baskets. "I believe," said Celtics guard Bill Sharman, "Red wanted us to see he wasn't about to back down from anything."

The Celtics, taking their cue from Auerbach, came away with a seven-game triumph for their first NBA championship. An injury to Russell the next year foiled their chances of repeating, but in 1959 they blitzed the Minneapolis Lakers

4-0 to became the first team ever to sweep an NBA Final. They won the title again in 1960, 1961, 1962, 1963, 1964, 1965, and 1966. Their string of eight titles in a row is unmatched in all major American professional sports. No one, not the New York Yankees in baseball or the Montreal Canadiens in hockey, had ever been able to do what the Celtics had done.

Throughout the dynasty, the Boston Celtics employed exactly two full-time front office employees: a public relations man and a secretary. All other tasks involved with running the team fell on the sloping shoulders of the coach. There was no general manager, no scouting department, no traveling secretary, and no assistant coaching staff. There was only Red Auerbach.

Auerbach was the man who put the team together, who kept the team together, and, year after year, who made sure that the team stayed hungry. Auerbach began the Celtics' training camp by asking his players, "Is this the year you're going to let down? Is this the year you're going to loaf?" He then whipped his players into shape by running the most grueling practices in the league. John Havlicek, a player renowned for his toughness and endurance, said of the practices, "Some days it was pure torture."

Auerbach wanted his players fit and he wanted them mean. "I used to tell my players: 'Basketball is like a war!'" Auerbach said. After the rigorous drills he would pit the Celtics against each other in scrimmages that often erupted into brawls. "We had a lot of fights in practice," said forward Satch Sanders, "and to us the games were usually a relief."

Auerbach kept the pressure on even after his agonizing training camps had gotten the Celtics off to a flying start. Auerbach motivated not by psychological mind games but by communicating his wishes forcefully, clearly, and directly. "You want smart, thinking ballplayers," he said. "Motivating can be so much easier if what you're saying appeals to their common sense and knowledge of the game."

That Auerbach's players proved themselves to be the smartest players in the league was no accident. "Red's great ability was to get everybody's head involved and to use ideas that the players would come up with," said forward Tommy Heinsohn. "In the last two minutes of a ball game, in the Celtics huddle—everybody thought Red was a tyrant—the first words out of his mouth would be 'Anybody got anything?' What that meant was that he trusted everybody that was playing for him to act like a coach and spot little things. We had five coaches on the floor."

The Celtics seemed to get stronger as the years went on. This also was no accident. Auerbach valued above all else the importance of keeping a team together. Each year, as other teams in the league changed personnel in a never-ending search for some magical combination, the Celtics stayed together and learned, more and more, how to move as one. "We knew how to use one another because we knew one another," said guard K. C. Jones.

Auerbach fit his players into roles perfectly

Auerbach is carried off the floor after winning the 1959 championship. From left to right are: K. C. Jones, Jim Loscutoff, Tommy Heinsohn, and Gene Conley. Jones and Heinsohn went on to become head coaches as well.

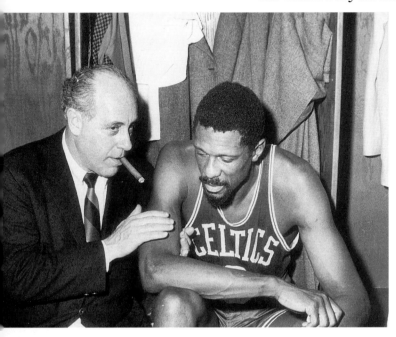

Auerbach shares a private moment with his top player, Bill Russell.

suited for their abilities and for the success of the team. Players like K. C. Jones, Sanders, and Russell dominated games on the defensive end, allowing scorers like Cousy, Heinsohn, Sam Jones, Havlicek, Sharman, and Frank Ramsey to do their damage on offense. Auerbach made sure that the scorers did not get more credit for victory than the defenders. He was especially careful in this regard with Russell, who he knew was by far the most important member of the team. He made sure that Russell was the highest-paid Celtic. He also knew that newspaper reporters and fans saw the flashy Cousy as the star of the team, so he talked up Russell's subtle yet fundamental contributions to anyone who would listen. "In that way, he balanced the egos," said Heinsohn.

Auerbach augmented the Celtics' ability to play as a team by using every kind of psychological edge he could think of. He began keeping one of his better players on the bench at the start of the game so that he could spring the man on the opposition just when they were starting to get tired. The so-called "sixth man" role, filled first by Frank Ramsey and then by John Havlicek, demoralized opponents who, said Auerbach, "found they had to work even harder just to keep up with us." Auerbach also used time-outs to send a demoralizing message to the opposition.

The Celtics, during a time-out, stood. "I wanted to show contempt for the other team," said Auerbach. "They had to sit down. They were tired. They had to rest."

Auerbach's most notorious way of crawling into the mind of the other team came near the end of a Celtics victory. It was then that the Celtics' coach would cease yelling at his players and harassing the referees. He would sit down and make himself comfortable on the bench and then he would light up a big, fat, odoriferous cigar. On more than one occasion, Frank Ramsey asked his coach, "Red, what if we lose?" Auerbach, taking a long puff, replied, "We're not going to lose."

They didn't. At the beginning of the 1965-66 season, the Celtics' coach announced that it would be his last year as a coach, adding, "You've got one more shot at Auerbach." The season, for the eighth time in a row, ended in a puff of smoke. With sixteen seconds left in game seven of the Finals, with the Celtics leading the Lakers by six, Massachusetts governor John Volpe did the honors of lighting yet another of Red's championship cigars.

4

PHIL JACKSON

T he chief Eastern Conference rival of Chuck Daly's Detroit Pistons during their championship years was not a team but a single man. This much was made abundantly clear in the 1989 Eastern Conference Finals. Just after a rare Piston playoff loss, the coach of the victorious team was asked to describe his strategy for the last-second shot that won the game. "Same as usual," replied Chicago Bulls coach Doug Collins with a smile. "Give the ball to Michael and get the hell out of the way."

It is hard to find fault with Collins's plan. The man he had rested the fate of the Bulls upon, Michael Jordan, was (and still is) arguably the best to ever play the game. But even the best player ever could not single-handedly beat a genuine team like the unified and multifaceted Pistons. After the Pistons topped the Bulls in six games, Collins was fired. Phil Jackson was

Phil Jackson confers with Michael Jordan.

named the new head coach of the Chicago Bulls.

The move did not go over well in Chicago. Collins was a fan favorite, and he had led a Bulls team to the conference finals for the first time in 14 years.

"I got tremendous heat," said General Manager Jerry Krause. "It was like I'd killed Christ." But Krause knew that he had in Collins' replacement the perfect man to lead the Bulls to an NBA championship. He knew that most coaches, like Collins (and like Stan Albeck and Kevin Loughery before him), would coach the Bulls as a one-man team. The prevailing attitude in the NBA was that the Bulls could never be anything more than a one-man team. Krause knew that Phil Jackson had the ability to see things in ways that other people couldn't. The new Bulls coach was not a normal NBA coach. Phil Jackson was different.

He'd always been different. As a reserve forward on Red Holzman's great Knicks teams, Jackson had distinguished himself both by his unique ability to defend against any player on the court, large or small, and by his refusal to conform to the ways of his fellow athletes off the court. He was the NBA's very own flower child, growing his hair long, wearing a beard, becoming a vegetarian, studying Eastern religion, pedaling through Manhattan traffic to Knicks games on a bicycle while his teammates rode in limousines, working on a Native American reservation in the off-season, experimenting with hallucinogenic drugs, and writing with unprecedented candor about all his bohemian adventures in his 1975 autobiography *Maverick*.

In the 1980s, Jackson became a head coach in the Continental Basketball Association (CBA).

He had learned the essentials of team play from Red Holzman, and in the CBA he learned how to communicate these essentials to a team. He learned, over several years in a league short on comforts and glory and long on insecurity and desperation, how to coach. When the Bulls gave him a chance he was ready, though critics of the coaching change made Jackson out to be some kind of whacked-out hippie.

The Bulls players knew that Phil Jackson could coach. Early in the 1988-89 season, Jackson had taken over a game that Collins had been tossed out of with the Bulls trailing by 14. Instead of panicking or (as the vociferous Collins would have done) inflicting on his struggling players a tongue-lashing, Jackson simply made one small defensive adjustment and told the team just to calm down and play their game. Power forward Horace Grant recalled, "It was like we were let out of a cage. We won the game because we were so relaxed, and we knew then that Phil should become the head coach."

Jackson's first order of business as head coach was to transform the Bulls from a one-man team to a five-man team that played as one. Jackson knew from his days as a reserve forward on the Knicks that there was nothing harder to stop than a team playing together. Jackson instituted an offense designed by Bulls assistant coach Tex Winter called the Triple-Post Offense. Unlike almost all current NBA offenses, which favor one-on-one and two-on-two isolation plays, the Triple-Post seeks to involve all five players in a flowing web of quick passes and hard cuts to the basket. "Tex's system is exactly what I was looking for," said Jackson. "When I got here, there was a feeling of impotence among some players who were eliminated from the process of ball movement."

Jackson's desire to involve more players in the offense did not cause him to lose sight of the most important member of the team. He knew that the only way his vision of the Bulls as a five-man team would come to pass would be if Jordan bought into Winter's offensive system. "It was a difficult sell to Michael," admitted Jackson.

Fortunately for the Bulls, Jordan was willing to give it a try. Jackson said, "More than anything, Mike wanted us to find a way to win. He knew other guys had to score. He was willing to make that sacrifice. But he had to see it work, had to have something to hang his hat on."

In Jackson's first year with the Bulls, Jordan's scoring average actually increased. But Jackson succeeded in making the other Bulls, notably burgeoning talents Horace Grant and Scottie Pippen, into vital cogs in the offense. The team upped its win total from 47 to 55 and extended the eventual champion Detroit Pistons to seven games in the Eastern Conference Finals. Throughout the playoffs, even the youngest of the Bulls had played with an unshakable confidence that belied their years. Jordan, for one, saw where this precocious poise was coming from. "Even though we might be in a pressure situation, we don't feel the pressure through the coach."

In 1990-91, Jackson's second season with the team, the Bulls seized the Central Division title from the Pistons, winning 61 games, and pummeled Detroit in four straight games to reach the NBA Finals. Under Jackson, the Bulls had become more of a team. Horace Grant blossomed into one of the league's best power forwards, role-players such as sweet-shooting John Paxson and big-bodied Bill Cartwright played to the utmost of their abilities, and small forward Scottie Pippen became a multi-talented star, leading the team in assists and blocked shots while finishing second in points, rebounds, and steals.

In the 1991 Finals, the Bulls, playing together, took a 3-1 lead over the Los Angeles Lakers. But in the fourth quarter of a tightly contested fifth game, Michael Jordan began to play as he had in the days before Jackson was his coach, like a man alone. He forced up five of the Bulls' first eight shots in the quarter before Jackson called time-out. Jackson calmly looked Jordan in the eye and asked, "Who's open?"

Two words were all the Bulls needed at that point. Jordan once again began hitting the open man—in this case Paxson, who drilled five fourth-quarter bombs—and the Bulls rolled to their first-ever NBA championship. The Bulls followed that success with a 67-15 record in 1991-92, the fourth-best regular-season record in NBA history, and added their second straight championship.

In the Finals the following year, the Phoenix Suns, led by Charles Barkley, appeared to be on the brink of sending the series to a seventh game, holding a two-point lead with 14 seconds left. Jackson's Bulls turned those 14 seconds into the defining moment of a dynasty. Every player

During his playing days, Jackson was known as a nonconformist. Few other pros have been known to take a bicycle to work.

on the floor for the Bulls touched the ball on their final possession, and though the desperate Suns scrambled to defend, they could not stop the five men that moved as one—a Bull was bound to come open, and he did. It was John Paxson, breaking free out beyond the three-point stripe. Horace Grant got him the ball and with time running out, Paxson swished a jumper to clinch the Bulls' third consecutive title.

Jackson (second from left) is a great motivator. Here he shares some thoughts with (from left to right) Will Perdue, Bill Cartwright, Scottie Pippen, and Michael Jordan at a team workout.

Jackson won the Coach of the Year award the following year when he led the Bulls to 55 wins without Michael Jordan, who had retired from basketball to flail at minor league curve balls. Jordan returned midway through the following year, rusty from his time away from the court, and the Bulls were stopped short of the NBA Finals for the second year in a row.

Dennis Rodman joined the Bulls the following year. Most NBA coaches, alarmed by Rodman's unpredictable and disruptive on- and off-court behavior, would have balked at having the tattooed rebounder join their team. Phil Jackson was different. He was the coach who lit incense to purge the Bulls' locker room of evil spirits, who led his team in Zen meditation, who gave each of his players a book to read during the season, who canceled a practice during a heated 1994 playoff matchup against the Knicks to take his team on a boat ride past the Statue of Liberty. Jackson's imaginative and original perspective on the world allowed him to see Rodman in a way that absolutely no one else in the NBA could. He compared him to a heyoka, a figure in Native American culture who wears bizarre clothes and walks backward while everyone else walks forward. "He was respected," Jackson pointed out, "because he brought a reality change."

Jackson had never been afraid of a reality change. He did not try to change Rodman but demanded from him a constant effort and a commitment to the team. Rodman responded with an outstanding year. The Bulls smashed the all-time record for wins in a season with 72 and beat the Sonics in the Finals to win their fourth title in six years.

Throughout the 1995-96 season the Bulls proved that not only were they no longer a one-man gang, but they were also one of the best teams ever to play the game. They hit the open man, they helped each other on defense, and when one man struggled, another man stepped up to carry the load. Even Michael Jordan was allowed to have an off night now and then. After a subpar performance in the deciding game of the 1996 Finals Jordan said, "My teammates were able to pull me through."

5

PAT RILEY

In the 1980s, the Greater Western Forum pulsed like a gigantic nightclub. Scantily clad dancers gyrated on the sidelines and Hollywood stars discoed in the stands. On the court, the man named Magic, often flashing his high-wattage smile, led a joyous and seemingly endless fast-breaking assault on the basket.

By the Lakers bench, a man stood and watched the dazzling show with an air of unshakable cool. At first glance, it would appear that this man, the coach of the Lakers, with his slicked-back hair and his impeccable Armani suit, fit in perfectly with the glitz and glamour of the rollicking spectacle unfolding all around him. Pat Riley, it seemed, was pure "showtime." But a closer look hinted at something else. The Los Angeles Lakers dominated pro basketball in the 1980s, and a closer look at Pat Riley revealed the raw, grisly heart beating at the center of this flamboyant, dominant team.

Pat Riley calls out a play for the Knicks during the 1994 NBA Finals.

Movie director Robert Towne was one of those who got a closer look. Upon meeting the Laker coach—and looking into his eyes—for the first time, he declared, "You're a desperate man, Riley." The coach did not deny it. Pat Riley was not showtime at all. Pat Riley was a street fighter. "I don't care what it is," said Gary Vitti, the Laker trainer. "Pat will scratch and claw. He will rip your eyes out."

Riley had not always been that way. When he was a young boy growing up in Schenectady, New York, in the 1950s, he wanted to take refuge from neighborhood bullies by hiding in the family garage. His father, Lee, a former professional baseball player, ordered Pat's older brothers to take the youngest Riley back to the place where he had been beaten up. Pat came home crying again and again. "I wanted to teach him not to be afraid," Lee Riley said. For the first time in his life, Riley was told by his father that there are times when a person has to make a stand.

By the time Pat Riley was a teenager, he was tough. A teammate on Riley's high school basketball team, Paul Heiner, remembered one pickup game in which Riley caught an elbow in the face and lost a tooth. "Pat walked to where the tooth was and kicked it off the court. And we kept playing," said Heiner. Riley showed his toughness again after entering the NBA and finding that his talent—which had made him a college star—did not match that of the majority of the players in the pros. But the street fighter managed to eke out a living for eight years in the league as a bench player by routinely outhustling and outpracticing everyone else on his team.

Riley never felt secure as a player, noting that "fear was my prime motivation." It was during one of the more anxious periods in his playing career that Riley saw his father for the last time. "In 1970, I'd just married Chris [Rodstrom] and was worried about my game," recalled Riley. "As my father was leaving the wedding reception, he stuck his head out of the car and said, 'Just remember, somewhere, someplace, sometime, you're going to have to plant your feet, make a stand, and kick some [butt]. And when that time comes, you do it.' It turned out those were his last words to me, because he died of a heart attack not long afterward."

After Riley's playing career came to an abrupt end in 1976, he plunged into a dark depression. He had no idea what to do with the rest of his life and spent his days building an eight-foot-high wall around his house in Brentwood, California. "I closed myself in," Riley said. "I was hiding my bitterness and rage." Just after Riley's demon-driven remodeling reached a climax of sorts—Riley waged a brief and fruitless attack on the house with a chainsaw—the ex-player was offered a job in broadcasting by Lakers play-by-play man Chick Hearn. Hearn, impressed by his new partner's knowledge of the game, encouraged Riley to give coaching a try.

Riley's meteoric rise to the top of the coaching world began when he took a job as an assistant to Lakers head coach Paul Westhead. In his first year in that capacity, the Lakers, led by Kareem Abdul-Jabbar and rookie sensation Magic Johnson, won the NBA title. By his third year, Riley had so impressed the Lakers' man-

As a player at the University of Kentucky and later in the pros, Riley wore his hair long and had a mustache and long sideburns—a far cry from the sharp suits and slicked-back hair he is famous for as a coach.

agement that he was asked to replace Westhead, under whom the Lakers had begun to struggle. Riley was at first extremely tentative as a head coach, and the Lakers, lacking necessary leadership, foundered. "They were waiting for me," said Riley of his players, "to put my foot down."

Riley put his foot down, railing at his players after a late-season loss to Chicago, and the Lakers put the pedal to the metal. Their new coach showed that he was the perfect man to lead them. "He's inventive. He makes good, quick decisions in games," observed Lakers general manager Jerry West. Riley also began using the motivational skills that would move guard Michael Cooper to say, "He'll show you something from that little box way inside that you only open up every once in a while." The inspired Lakers, unleashing the fast-break offense that made opponents seem as if they were playing in cement sneakers, streaked to the 1982 NBA crown.

The Lakers were swept in the Finals the following year by Moses Malone and the Philadelphia 76ers. The disappointment of this defeat was exceeded a year later when the favored Lakers were beaten by a gutsy, resourceful Boston Celtic squad in a classic seven-game series. In that series, Larry Bird and his Celtic mates were the street fighters. They took the best that the Lakers could dish out and kept coming until the very spirit of the showtime team was snapped. The Celtics won because they were tougher.

This did not sit well with Pat Riley. Gary Vitti recalled the beginning of the following season, saying, "Pat was screwed down pretty tight, like a spring. And it escalated from there." The Lakers won 62 games and tore through their first three opponents in the playoffs to reach the

Finals. The Celtics were there and they were ready. Bird's team thrashed the Lakers in Game 1, 148-114. "We really weren't sure of ourselves," said forward James Worthy. "We got back to the Finals and said, 'Golly, we got the Celtics again. How're we gonna do it?'"

As Worthy's coach took a seat on the bus that would take the Lakers to the Boston Garden for Game 2, his mind reeled with questions: How are we gonna do it? How are we going to finally beat the Celtics? The questions gnawing at Riley gradually became more and more basic, more and more fundamental. In the end there was only one question for Riley and the Lakers: Who are we and what are we made of?

Abdul-Jabbar, the grizzled Lakers captain who had struggled badly in the first game, boarded the bus with his father, Al Alcindor. "And as I watched them together," Riley recalled, "I began to think of fathers, of my father." Riley had not seen his father in 15 years. "But as I sat in that bus," said Riley, "I heard that voice again." With that voice came the answer.

In the Lakers' locker room before tip-off, Riley told his team of the voice he heard on the bus. He told them of how his father had made him face up to bullies when he had been a kid and how his father had reminded him as an adult, in his last words to him, that everyone, sometime, somewhere, has to take a stand. He told his team that this was the place and now was the time. He said, "So let us all take that stand."

The fired-up Lakers took the court like a gang of desperate street fighters and seized control of the series with a gritty 109-102 win. "That set the tone," said Worthy. "That game was the turning point in Laker history." The Lakers went on

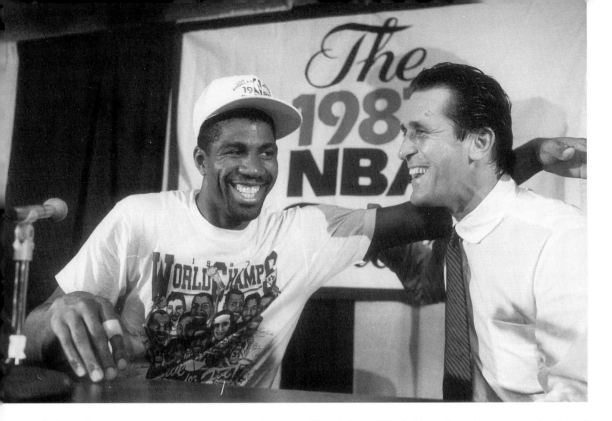

Riley shares a joyous moment with Magic Johnson after winning the 1987 championship.

to win the 1985 NBA title in six games behind the miraculously rejuvenated Abdul-Jabbar. It was the first time in eight tries that a Lakers team had beaten a Celtics team in the Finals. Two years later, when the Celtics and Lakers met to decide the 1987 NBA championship, Riley's team won again.

The hungry look in Pat Riley's eyes remained. He did not want his team, as they had done after each of their previous championships, to suffer a mental letdown the following year. No team had repeated as league champion since Bill Russell's Celtics in 1969. Riley was asked—as the champagne was still flowing in the Lakers' victorious locker room—whether he thought the Lakers could repeat. He said without pause, "I guarantee it."

The pressure on the Laker players that this quote instantly produced was augmented by

Riley throughout the following season. He refused to let up on his players for a moment, and this dogged prodding, though increasingly resented by the players, proved to be the only way for the long-time hex on repeating to be broken. After the Lakers had become not only the first team to repeat as champions in 18 years, but also the first team to ever win three seven-game playoff series in a single year, guard Byron Scott said of Riley, "He pretty much got it all out of us that year."

Riley's relentless motivational tactics began to wear thin on the Laker players in the following years. An early exit from the 1990 playoffs spelled the swan song for Riley in Los Angeles and, after a year away from coaching, Riley became the head coach of the New York Knicks.

The physical, defensive-minded Knicks reflected the combative nature of their coach more than the flashy, artful Lakers ever had. Some lauded the hustle and desire displayed by the over-achieving Knicks, who were far from the most talented team in the league. Others criticized the win-at-all-costs attitude of Riley's team, as well as their knack of turning games into slow-paced wrestling matches. Chicago Bulls coach Phil Jackson bluntly declared, "The Knicks play ugly."

The Knicks, ugly or not, won their share of games. In 1993-94, their best season, they came within a John Starks jump shot of beating the Houston Rockets to win the NBA championship. The following year, after the Knicks were ousted by the Indiana Pacers in the second round of the playoffs, Riley abandoned the Knicks to become the head coach of the Miami Heat.

The abrupt departure from New York was generally portrayed as the self-serving act of a Machi-

Riley answers questions from the press prior to the seventh game of the 1994 NBA Finals.

avellian cutthroat. Riley's reputation was further sullied when one of his players, a strapping goon named Matt Geiger, flagrantly fouled Orlando Magic center Shaquille O'Neal in a preseason game, breaking the rap star's thumb. "That was our game plan," Geiger said. "If Shaq got it down low, put a good foul on him." Geiger's teammate Stacey King added, "We will put it in the back of our opponents' minds, 'When I go to the hole, somebody will hammer me.'" The Heat's strategy, obviously authored by Riley, provoked disgust in many quarters. "Riley is taking the league down the sewer with this stuff," wrote Rick Reilly in *Sports Illustrated*.

Riley ignored the criticism. He had said earlier in his career, "If you go about living your life as you choose, and you're happy with it, then the opinion makers will never really affect you." The talent-thin Heat made the playoffs in 1996, and the following season they won the Atlantic Division. On the sidelines, the man with the slicked-back hair and the Armani suit watched, his eyes still the eyes of a street fighter.

6

LENNY WILKENS

Throughout the first nine seasons of his Hall-of-Fame playing career, Lenny Wilkens treated every kind of pressure that came his way the same. He ignored it. His myriad clutch performances and his indestructible poker face made it seem as if he could dribble a ball across a mine field without getting rattled. Then, in 1969, he became the head coach of the Seattle Super-Sonics while remaining on the roster as a player. During the early days of that season, Lenny Wilkens began to look as if the pressure was getting to him. He began to look, in other words, like a regular NBA coach.

"His entire face would look like a hand closing into a fist—his forehead, his eyes, his jaw," remembered his assistant coach that year, Tom Meschery. Meschery's boss was only the second black man to coach an NBA team. And though

Ken Norman carries a banner that celebrates Lenny Wilkens's passing of Red Auerbach for most career wins as a coach.

Bill Russell, who had been the first, had coached the Celtics to back-to-back championships, there still persisted a racist belief that blacks, even men like Wilkens who had excelled as players, did not have the mental capabilities to coach. Wilkens, a fiercely proud man, wanted to instantly shatter this myth. But winning with the Super-Sonics that year was not easy, especially considering the fact that the only dependable player on an otherwise lackluster roster was a point guard named Lenny Wilkens. As the losses mounted, Wilkens, for the first and only time in his long career in basketball, began to take the game home with him.

It was after one loss that Wilkens overheard his wife on the phone canceling plans to have dinner with friends. She explained that her husband was simply too distraught to see anyone. Hearing that convinced Wilkens that enough was enough. "I couldn't let basketball eat up my life," he said. "It just wasn't fair to the people I loved. How could I be gone for two weeks on a road trip, then come home and do that to my wife? In the scale of life, what's important? My belief in God. My family. And being accountable for who I am. If these three things are in place, all other things are attainable."

With that realization, one of the greatest coaching careers in NBA history began in earnest. Wilkens, still going strong in a coaching career that has spanned four decades, stands alone now for both his stellar coaching record (he is the NBA's all-time career leader in wins) and his ability to keep the mercurial fortunes of the game from clouding his judgment of what's important. Doug Collins, the coach of the Detroit Pistons, found himself talking about this aspect of Lenny

Wilkens when describing the stress of an NBA coaching job. "It's insidious because you don't even realize what coaching is doing to you and your life until you are in very deep. That is why I've always admired Lenny Wilkens, and how he has kept his perspective. He's a rare one."

Wilkens grew up in the poor Bedford-Stuyvesant section of Brooklyn. His father died when he was four, and by the time he was seven he was working to help keep food on the table. He was sent by his mother to a Catholic high school, and there he began experiencing the kind of racism that would follow him throughout his life. "There were people looking at me like I was some kind of insect. People who assumed that because I was from Bed-Stuy, I was carrying a knife or a gun."

Wilkens devoted himself to excelling in the classroom. "Education breaks down stereotypes," he said. "Understand, it was not a vindictive-type thing with me. But I was aware that I was going to have to change people's minds. I wanted to prove I was as intelligent as anyone else."

His intelligence carried over to the basketball court. Wilkens starred at Providence College before joining the NBA as a member of the St. Louis Hawks in 1960. St. Louis was still the southernmost city in the league, and, as in much of the South at that time, there was still an abundance of overtly racist practices. Wilkens was not allowed to eat at the restaurant just across the street from the Hawks' arena. This infuriated him. "I was demoralized by this. I had spent my whole life in the Northeast, and it had never happened to me before. I couldn't help but take this personally. I was college-educated, I had worked hard my whole life, I had accomplished

As a pro player, Wilkens was known as one of the smartest and smoothest point guards ever.

far more than those people who were telling me that I wasn't good enough to eat in their lousy restaurant. I was both angry and embarrassed, and I just left."

Wilkens did not let such things prevent him from becoming one of the best point guards in NBA history. "Lenny Wilkens was different," said the Hawks' broadcaster, Jerry Gross. "He made the other guys look better."

Great success eluded Wilkens in the first few years of his coaching career. The SuperSonics lacked the kind of talent needed to win games, and the Portland Trailblazers, whom Wilkens coached from 1974-76, were wracked by injuries. Wilkens returned to Seattle as director of player development in 1977. He helped assemble a team that, at the beginning of the 1977-78 season, looked like one of the worst teams ever put on an NBA floor. "We were a calamity of misfits," said Seattle guard Freddy Brown. But Wilkens knew that his players could play, and when he was chosen to replace Bob Hopkins—after Seattle started the season at 5-17—he got the team going. Wilkens began to emphasize the strengths of the SuperSonic roster, their guards. With Gus Williams, "Downtown" Freddy Brown, and a previously unknown guard named Dennis Johnson leading the way, the SuperSonics took off.

It was a team without stars but with incredible balance. They also played with a fire that had been completely lacking before Wilkens took over, and it made them instantly into one of the most hard-working teams in the league. Wilkens had put this fire into the team. "The team was badly in need of confidence. Mentally they were whipped. They were in a bottomless pit. I told them they did have talent. That I had confidence in them."

The Sonics got all the way to the NBA Finals that year in what was the biggest mid-season turnaround in the history of the league. They lost to the Washington Bullets in seven games but returned to the Finals the following year to sweep the Bullets and win their first-ever NBA championship.

In 1986, Wilkens joined the Cleveland Cavaliers, and within two years he turned the most

The reason why coaches coach: Wilkens holds the trophy for winning the world championship in 1979 with the Seattle Supersonics.

inept franchise in the league into a 57-game winner. The Cavaliers not only won, but they also won in a classy way, with balanced scoring, tough defense, and intelligence. Wilkens' players played hard and they played smart.

Widespread public acclaim eluded the understated, no-frills Cleveland coach. But Wilkens's peers knew what he could do for a team. "There's no doubt Lenny is a great coach," Chuck Daly said. "He knows the game, he knows how to teach—he can coach in any era." Another Hall-of-Fame coach, Red Auerbach, said, "People think because Lenny is low-key that you can step on him. Nobody pushes him around."

By 1994, Wilkens's teams had been winning for so long that it was no longer possible to ignore his coaching abilities. In his first year as head coach of the Atlanta Hawks, Wilkens finally won a long overdue Coach of the Year award. The trophy that Wilkens received, as if to foreshadow forthcoming events, was a depiction of the coach who served the league as the standard of excellence in coaching, the rumpled bald guy with a cigar, Red Auerbach. Wilkens met that standard of excellence again the following year. On January 6, 1995, the Hawks defeated the Washington Bullets 112-90, giving Wilkens his 939th career regular-season coaching victory. With that he passed Auerbach, who had 938 wins, to become the new all-time leader in coaching victories. Auerbach, always an admirer of Wilkens, was in attendance, and Wilkens paid tribute to him, smoking a victory cigar and saying, "Red is a legend, so this a huge achievement. When I started coaching, all of us looked at Red and thought his record was something that would stand forever. The satisfaction is that only one person can be Number One at a time. Only one guy can be at the top. It's nice to be there, for however long. I got there, and no one can take that away from me."

STATISTICS

RED AUERBACH

YEAR	TEAM	REC	PCT
1950-51	Bos	39-30	.565
1951-52	Bos	39-27	.591
1952-53	Bos	46-25	.648
1953-54	Bos	42-30	.583
1954-55	Bos	36-36	.500
1955-56	Bos	39-33	.542
1956-57	Bos	44-28	.611
1957-58	Bos	49-23	.681
1958-59	Bos	52-20	.722
1959-60	Bos	59-16	.787
1960-61	Bos	57-22	.722
1961-62	Bos	60-20	.750
1962-63	Bos	58-22	.725
1963-64	Bos	59-21	.738
1964-65	Bos	62-18	.775
1965-66	Bos	54-26	.675
Totals		795-397	.667

PHIL JACKSON

YEAR	TEAM	REC	PCT
1989-90	Chi	55-27	.671
1990-91	Chi	61-21	.744
1991-92	Chi	67-15	.817
1992-93	Chi	57-25	.695
1993-94	Chi	55-27	.671
1994-95	Chi	47-35	.573
1995-96	Chi	72-10	.878
1996-97	Chi	69-13	.841
Totals		483-173	.736

LENNY WILKENS

YEAR	TEAM	REC	PCT
1969-70	Sea	36-46	.440
1970-71	Sea	38-44	.463
1971-72	Sea	47-35	.573
1974-75	Port	38-44	.463
1975-76	Port	37-45	.451
1977-78	Sea	42-18	.700
1978-79	Sea	52-30	.634
1979-80	Sea	56-26	.683
1980-81	Sea	34-48	.415
1981-82	Sea	52-30	.634
1982-83	Sea	48-34	.585
1983-84	Sea	42-40	.512
1984-85	Sea	31-51	.378
1986-87	Cle	31-51	.378
1987-88	Cle	42-40	.512
1988-89	Cle	57-25	.695
1989-90	Cle	42-40	.512
1990-91	Cle	33-49	.402
1991-92	Cle	57-25	.695
1992-93	Cle	54-28	.659
1993-94	Atl	57-25	.695
1994-95	Atl	42-40	.512
1995-96	Atl	46-36	.561
1996-97	Atl	56-26	.683
Totals		1070-870	.552

PAT RILEY

YEAR	TEAM	REC	PCT
1981-82	LA	50-21	.704
1982-83	LA	58-24	.707
1983-84	LA	54-28	.659
1984-85	LA	62-20	.756
1985-86	LA	62-20	.756
1986-87	LA	65-17	.793
1987-88	LA	62-20	.756
1988-89	LA	57-25	.695
1989-90	LA	63-19	.768
1991-92	NY	51-31	.622
1992-93	NY	60-22	.732
1993-94	NY	57-25	.695
1994-95	NY	55-27	.671
1995-96	Mia	42-40	.512
1996-97	Mia	61-21	.744
TOTALS		859-360	.705

COACHES OF THE YEAR

1962-63 Harry Gallatin, St. Louis

1963-64 Alex Hannum, San Francisco

1964-65 Red Auerbach, Boston

1965-66 Dolph Schayes, Philadelphia

1966-67 Johnny Kerr, Chicago

1967-68 Richie Guerin, St. Louis

1968-69 Gene Shue, Baltimore

1969-70 Red Holzman, New York

1970-71 Dick Motta, Chicago

1971-72 Bill Sharman, Los Angeles

1972-73 Tom Heinsohn, Boston

1973-74 Ray Scott, Detroit

1974-75 Phil Johnson, KC-Omaha

1975-76 Bill Fitch, Cleveland

1976-77 Tom Nissalke, Houston

1977-78 Hubie Brown, Atlanta

1978-79 Cotton Fitzsimmons, Kansas City

1979-80 Bill Fitch, Boston

1980-81 Jack McKinney, Indiana

1981-82 Gene Shue, Washington

1982-83 Don Nelson, Milwaukee

1983-84 Frank Layden, Utah

1984-85 Don Nelson, Milwaukee

1985-86 Mike Fratello, Atlanta

1986-87 Mike Schuler, Portland

1987-88 Doug Moe, Denver

1988-89 Cotton Fitzsimmons, Phoenix

1989-90 Pat Riley, LA Lakers

1990-91 Don Chaney, Houston

1991-92 Don Nelson, Golden State

1992-93 Pat Riley, New York

1993-94 Lenny Wilkens, Atlanta

1994-95 Del Harris, LA Lakers

1995-96 Phil Jackson, Chicago

1996-97 Pat Riley, Miami

This award was named
the Arnold "Red" Auerbach Trophy in 1986

FURTHER READING

Auerbach, Red, with Joe Fitzgerald. *On and Off the Court.* New York: Macmillan, 1985.

Hoffer, Richard. "Sitting Bull." *Sports Illustrated,* May 27, 1996.

Holzman, Red, with Leonard Lewin. *My Unforgettable Season: 1970.* New York: Tom Doherty Associates, 1993.

Lazenby, Roland. *The Lakers: A Basketball Journey.* New York: St. Martin's Press, 1993.

Lupica, Mike. "The Wayne and Lenny Show." *Esquire,* June 1989.

Pluto, Terry. *Falling From Grace.* New York: Simon and Schuster, 1995.

Pluto, Terry. *Tall Tales.* New York: Simon and Schuster, 1992.

Sampson, Curt. *Full Court Pressure.* New York: Doubleday, 1995.

Shaughnessy, Dan. *Ever Green: The Boston Celtics.* New York: St. Martin's Press, 1990.

ABOUT THE AUTHOR

Josh Wilker is the author of several books for young readers, including biographies of Wayne Gretzky and A. J. Foyt. He played small forward for the 1987-88 Johnson State College Badgers and now makes his home in New York City.

INDEX